MARXISM VS. LIBERALISM

AN INTERVIEW

By

H. G. WELLS & J. V. STALIN

British Library Cataloguing-in-Publication Data
A catalogue record for this book is available from
the British Library

H. G. Wells

Herbert George Wells was born in Bromley, England in 1866. He apprenticed as a draper before becoming a pupil-teacher at Midhurst Grammar School in West Sussex. Some years later, Wells won a scholarship to the School of Science in London, where he developed a strong interest in biology and evolution, founding and editing the *Science Schools Journal*. However, he left before graduating to return to teaching, and began to focus increasingly on writing. His first major essay on science, 'The Rediscovery of the Unique', appeared in 1891. However, it was in 1895 that Wells seriously established himself as a writer, with the publication of the now iconic novel, *The Time Machine*.

Wells followed *The Time Machine* with the equally well-received *War of the Worlds* (1898), which proved highly popular in the USA, and was serialized in the magazine *Cosmopolitan*. Around the turn of the century, he also began to write extensively on politics, technology and the future, producing works *The Discovery of the Future* (1902) and *Mankind in the Making* (1903). An active socialist, in 1904 Wells joined the Fabian Society, and his 1905 book *A Modern Utopia* presented a vision of a socialist society founded on reason and compassion. Wells also penned a range of successful comic novels, such as *Kipps* (1905) and *The History of Mr Polly* (1910).

Wells' 1920 work, *The Outline of History,* was penned in response to the Russian Revolution, and declared that world would be improved by education, rather than revolution. It made Wells one of the most important political thinkers of the twenties and thirties, and he began to write for a number of journals and newspapers, even travelling to Russia to lecture Lenin and Trotsky on social reform. Appalled by the carnage of World War II, Wells began to work on a project dealing with the perils of nuclear war, but died before completing it. He is now regarded as one of the greatest science-fiction writers of all time, and an important political thinker.

H.G. Wells visited the Soviet Union in 1934 and on July 23 he interviewed Joseph Stalin. The conversation, lasting from 4 P.M. to 6:50 P.M., was recorded by Constantine Oumansky, then head of the Press Bureau of the Commissariat of Foreign Affairs. The text, as printed in this pamphlet, has been approved by Mr. Wells.

"MARXISM VS. LIBERALISM"
TWO-CENT PAMPHLET EDITION

Wells: I am very much obliged to you, Mr. Stalin, for agreeing to see me. I was in the United States recently. I had a long conversation With President Roosevelt and tried to ascertain what his leading ideas were. Now I have come to you to ask you what you are doing to change the world....

Stalin: Not so very much....

Wells: I wander around the world as a common man and, as a common man, observe what is going on around me.

Stalin: Important public men like yourself are not "common men." Of course, history alone can show how important this or that public man has been; at all events you do not look at the world as a "common man."

Wells: I am not pretending humility. What I mean is that I try to see the world through the eyes of the common man, and not as a party politician or a responsible administrator. My visit to the United States excited my mind. The old financial world is collapsing; the economic life of the country is being reorganized on new lines. Lenin said: "We must learn to do business," learn this from the capitalists. Today the capitalists have to learn from you, to grasp the spirit of socialism. It seems to me that what is taking place in the United States is a profound reorganization, the creation of planned, that is, socialist, economy. You and Roosevelt begin from two different starting points. But is there not a relation in ideas, a kinship of ideas, between Washington and Moscow? In Washington I was struck by the same thing I see going on here; they are building offices, they are creating a number of new state regulation bodies, they are organizing a long-needed Civil Service. Their need, like yours, is directive ability.

Stalin: The United States is pursuing a different aim from that which we are pursuing in the U.S.S.R. The aim which the Americans are pursuing arose out of the economic troubles, out of the economic crisis. The Americans want to rid themselves of the crisis on the basis of private capitalist activity without changing the economic basis. They are trying to reduce to a minimum the ruin, the losses caused by the existing economic system. Here, however, as you know, in place of the old destroyed economic basis an entirely different, a new economic basis has been created. Even if the Americans you mention partly achieve their aim, i.e., reduce these losses to a minimum, they will not destroy the roots of the anarchy which is inherent in the existing capitalist system. They are preserving the economic system which must inevitably lead, and cannot but lead, to anarchy in production. Thus, at best, it will be a matter, not of the reorganization of society, not of abolishing the old social system which gives rise to anarchy and crises, but of restricting certain of its bad features, restricting certain of its excesses. Subjectively, perhaps, these Americans think they are reorganizing society; objectively, however, they are preserving the present basis of society. That is why, objectively, there will be no reorganization of society.

Nor will there be planned economy. What is planned economy? What are some of its attributes? Planned economy tries to abolish unemployment. Let us suppose it is possible, while preserving the capitalist system, to reduce unemployment to a certain minimum. But surely, no capitalist would ever agree to the complete abolition of unemployment, to the abolition of the reserve army of unemployed, the purpose of which is to bring pressure on the labor market, to ensure a supply of cheap labor. Here you have one of the rents in the "planned economy" of bourgeois society. Furthermore, planned economy presupposes increased output in those branches of industry which produce goods that the masses of the people need particularly. But you know that the expansion of production under capitalism takes place for entirely different motives, that capital flows into those branches of economy in which the rate of profit is highest. You will never compel a capitalist to incur loss to himself and agree to a lower rate of profit for the sake of satisfying the needs of the people. Without getting rid of the capitalists, without abolishing the principle of private property in the means of production, it is impossible to create planned economy.

Wells: I agree with much of what you have said. But I would like to stress the point that if a country as a whole adopts the principle of planned economy, if the government, gradually, step by step, begins consistently to apply this principle, the financial oligarchy will at last be abolished and socialism, in the Anglo-Saxon meaning of the word, will be brought about. The effect of the ideas of Roosevelt's "New Deal" is most powerful, and in my opinion they are socialist ideas. It seems to me that instead of stressing the antagonism between the two worlds, we should, in the present circumstances, strive to establish a common tongue for all the constructive forces.

Stalin: In speaking of the impossibility of realizing the principles of planned economy while preserving the economic basis of capitalism I do not in the least desire to belittle the outstanding personal qualities of Roosevelt, his initiative, courage, and determination. Undoubtedly Roosevelt stands out as one of the strongest figures among all the captains of the contemporary capitalist world. That is why I would like once again to emphasize the point that my conviction that planned economy is impossible under the conditions of capitalism does not mean that I have any doubts about the personal abilities, talent, and courage of President Roosevelt. But if the circumstances are unfavorable, the most talented captain cannot reach the goal you refer to. Theoretically, of course, the possibility of marching gradually, step by step, under the conditions of capitalism, towards the goal which you call socialism in the Anglo-Saxon meaning of the word, is not precluded. But what will this "socialism" be? At best, bridling to some extent the most unbridled of individual representatives of capitalist profit, some increase in the application of the principle of regulation in national economy. That is all very well. But as soon as Roosevelt, or any other captain in the contemporary bourgeois world, proceeds to undertake something serious against the foundation of capitalism, he will inevitably suffer utter defeat.

The banks, the industries, the large enterprises, the large farms are not in Roosevelt's hands. All these are private property. The railroads, the mercantile fleet, all these belong to private owners. And finally, the army of skilled workers, the engineers, the technicians, these too are not at Roosevelt's command, they are at the command of the private owners; they all work for the private owners. We must not forget the functions of the State in the bourgeois world. The State is an institution that organizes the defense of the country, organizes the maintenance of "order"; it is an apparatus for collecting taxes. The capitalist State does not deal much with economy in the strict sense of the word; the latter is not in the hands of the State. On the contrary, the State is in the hands of capitalist economy. That is why I fear that, in spite of all his energy and abilities, Roosevelt will not achieve the goal you mention, if indeed that is his goal. Perhaps, in the course of several generations, it will be possible to approach this goal somewhat; but I personally think that even this is not very probable.

Wells: Perhaps I believe more strongly in the economic interpretation of politics than you do. Huge forces driving towards better organization, for the better functioning of the community, that is, for socialism, have been brought into action by invention and modern science. Organization, and the regulation of individual action, have become mechanical necessities, irrespective of social theories. If we begin with the State control of the banks. and then follow with the control of transport, of the heavy industries, of industry in general, of commerce, etc., such an all- embracing control will be equivalent to the State ownership of all branches of national economy. This will be the process of socialization. Socialism and individualism are not opposites like black and white. There are many intermediate stages between them. There is individualism that borders on brigandage, and there is discipline and organization that are the equivalent of socialism. The introduction of planned economy depends, to a large degree, upon the organizers of economy, upon the skilled technical intelligentsia, who, step by step, can be converted to the socialist principles of organization. And this is the most important thing. Because organization comes before socialism. It is the more important fact. Without organization the socialist idea is a mere idea.

Stalin: There is no, nor should there be, irreconcilable contrast between the individual and the collective, between the interests of the individual person and the interests of the collective, There should be no such contrast, because collectivism, socialism, does not deny, but combines individual interests with the interests of the collective. Socialism cannot abstract itself from individual interests. Socialist society alone can most fully satisfy these personal interests. More than that; socialist society alone can firmly safeguard the interests of the individual.

In this sense there is no irreconcilable contrast between "individualism" and socialism. But can we deny the contrast between classes, between the propertied class, the capitalist class, and the toiling class, the proletarian class? On the one hand we have the propertied class which owns the banks, the factories, the mines, transport, the plantations in colonies. These people see nothing but their own interests, their striving after profits. They do not submit to the will of the collective; they strive to subordinate every collective to their will. On the other hand we have the class of the poor, the exploited Class, which owns neither factories nor works, nor banks, which is compelled to live by selling its labor power to the capitalists and which lacks the opportunity to satisfy its most elementary requirements. How can such opposite interests and strivings be reconciled? As far as I know, Roosevelt has not succeeded in finding the path of conciliation between these interests. And it is impossible, as experience has shown. Incidentally, you know the situation in the United States better than I do as I have never been there and I watch American affairs mainly from literature. But I have some experience in fighting for socialism and this experience tells me that if Roosevelt makes a real attempt to satisfy the interests of the proletarian class at the expense of the capitalist class, the latter will put another president in his place. The capitalists will say: Presidents come and presidents go, but we go on forever; if this or that president does not protect our interests, we shall find another. What can the president oppose to the will of the capitalist class?

Wells: I object to this simplified classification of mankind into poor and rich. Of course there is a category of people which strives only for profit. But are not these people regarded as nuisances in the West just as much as here? Are there not plenty of people in the West for whom profit is not an end, who own a certain amount of wealth, who want to invest and obtain a profit from this investment, but who do not regard this as the main object? They regard investment as an inconvenient necessity. Are there not plenty of capable and devoted engineers, organizers of industry, whose activities are stimulated by something other than profit? In my opinion there is a numerous class of capable people who admit that the present system is unsatisfactory. and who are destined to playa great role in future socialist society. During the past few years I have been much engaged in and have thought of the need for conducting propaganda in favor of socialism and cosmopolitanism among wide circles of engineers, airmen, military-technical people, etc. It is useless approaching these circles with two track class war propaganda. These people understand the condition of the world. They understand that it is a bloody muddle, but they regard your simple classwar antagonism as nonsense.

Stalin: You object to the simplified classification of mankind into rich and poor. Of course there is a middle stratum, there is the technical intelligentsia that you have mentioned and among which there are very good and very honest people. Among them there are also dishonest and wicked people, there are all sorts of people among them. But first of all mankind is divided into. rich and poor, into property owners and exploited; and to abstract oneself from this fundamental division and from the antagonism between poor and rich means abstracting oneself from the fundamental fact. I do not deny the existence of intermediate, middle strata, which either take the side of one or other of these two conflicting classes, or else take up a neutral or semineutral position in this struggle. But, I repeat, to abstract oneself from this fundamental division in society and from the fundamental struggle between the two main classes means ignoring facts. This struggle is going on and will continue. The outcome of the struggle will be determined by the proletarian class, the working class.

Wells: But are there not many people who are not poor, but who work and work productively? .

Stalin: Of course, there are small landowners, artisans, small traders, but it is not these people who decide the fate of a country, but the toiling masses, who produce all the things society requires.

Wells: But there are very different kinds of capitalists. There are capitalists who only think about profit, about getting rich; but there are also those who are prepared to make sacrifices. Take old Morgan for example. He only thought about profit; he was a parasite on society, simply, he merely accumulated wealth. But take Rockefeller. He is a brilliant organizer; he has set an example of how to organize the delivery of oil that is worthy of emulation. Or take Ford. Of course Ford is selfish.

But is he not a passionate organizer of rationalized production from whom you take lessons? I would like to emphasize the fact that recently an important change in opinion towards the U.S.S.R. has taken place in English speaking countries. The reason for this, first of all, is the position of Japan and the events in Germany. But there are other reasons besides those arising from international politics. There is a more profound reason, namely, the recognition by many people of the fact that the system based on private profit is breaking down. Under these circumstances, it seems to me, we must not bring to the forefront the antagonism between the two worlds, but should strive to combine all the constructive movements, all the constructive forces in one line as much as possible. It seems to me that I am more to the Left than you, Mr. Stalin; I think the old system is nearer to its end than you think.

Stalin: In speaking of the capitalists who strive only for profit, only to get rich, I do not want to say that these are the most worthless people, capable of nothing else. Many of them undoubtedly possess great organizing talent, Which I do not dream of denying. We Soviet people learn a great deal from the capitalists. And Morgan, whom you characterize so unfavorably, was undoubtedly a good, capable organizer. But if you mean people who are prepared to reconstruct the world, of course, you will not be able to find them in the ranks of those who faithfully serve the cause of profit. We and they stand at opposite poles. You mentioned Ford. Of course, he is a capable organizer of production. But don't you know his attitude towards the working class? Don't you know how many workers he throws on the street? The capitalist is riveted to profit; and no power on earth can tear him away from it. Capitalism will be abolished, not, by "organizers" of production, not by the technical intelligentsia, but by the working class, because the aforementioned strata do not play an independent role. The engineer, the organizer of production, does not work as he would like to, but as he is ordered, in such a way as to serve the interests of his employers. There are exceptions of course; there are people in this stratum who have awakened from the intoxication of capitalism the technical intelligentsia can, under certain conditions, perform miracles and greatly benefit mankind. But It can also cause great harm. We Soviet people have not a little experience of the technical intelligentsia. After the October Revolution, a certain section of the technical intelligentsia refused to take part in the work of constructing the new society; they opposed this work of construction and sabotaged it. We did all we possibly could to bring the technical intelligentsia into this work of construction we tried this way and that. Not a little time passed before our technical intelligentsia agreed actively to assist the new system. Today the best section of this technical intelligentsia are in the front rank of the builders of socialist society. Having this experience, we are far from underestimating the good and the bad sides of the technical intelligentsia and we know that on the one hand it can do harm, and on the other hand, it can perform "miracles." Of course, things would be different if it were possible, at one stroke, spiritually to tear the technical intelligentsia away from the capitalist world. But that is utopia. Are there many of the technical intelligentsia who would dare break away from the bourgeois world and set to work to reconstruct society? Do you think there are many people of this kind, say, in England or in France? No, there are few who would be willing to break away from their employers and begin reconstructing the world. Besides, can we lose sight of the fact that in order to transform the world it is necessary'to have political power? It seems to me, Mr. Wells, that you greatly underestimate the question of political power, that it entirely drops out of your conception. What can those, even with the best intentions in the world, do if they are unable to raise the question of seizing power, and do not possess power? At best they can help the class which takes power, but they cannot change the world themselves. This can only be done by a great class which will take the place of the capitalist class and become the sovereign master as the latter was before. This class is the working class. Of course, the assistance of the technical intelligentsia must be accepted; and the latter, in turn, must be assisted. But it must not be thought that the technical intelligentsia can play an independent historical role. The transformation of the world is a great, complicated and painful process. For this great task a great class is required. Big ships go on long voyages.

Wells: Yes, but for long voyages a captain and a navigator are required.

Stalin: That is true; but what is first required for a long voyage is a big ship. What is a navigator without a ship? An idle man.

Wells: The big ship is humanity, not a class.

Stalin: You, Mr. Wells, evidently start out with the assumption that all men are good. I, however, do not forget that there are many wicked men. I do not believe in the goodness of the bourgeoisie.

Wells: I remember the situation with regard to the technical intelligentsia several decades ago. At that time the technical intelligentsia was numerically small, but there was much to do and every engineer, technician and intellectual found his opportunity. That is why the technical intelligentsia was the least revolutionary class. Now, however, there is a superabundance of technical intellectuals, and their mentality has changed very sharply. The skilled man, who would formerly never listen to revolutionary talk, is now greatly interested in it. Recently I was dining with the Royal Society, our great English scientific society. The President's speech was a speech for social planning and scientific control. Thirty years ago, they would not have listened to what I say to them now. Today, the man at the head of the Royal Society holds revolutionary views and insists on the scientific reorganization of human society. Mentality changes. Your class-war propaganda has not. kept pace with these facts.

Stalin: Yes, I know this, and this is to be explained by the fact that capitalist society is now in a cul-de-sac. The capitalists are seeking, but cannot find, a way out of this cul-de-sac that would be compatible with the dignity of this class, compatible with the interests of this class. They could, to some extent, crawl out of the crisis on their hands and knees, but they cannot find an exit that would enable them to walk out of it with head raised high, a way out that would not. fundamentally disturb the interests of capitalism. This, of course, is realized by wide circles of the technical intelligentsia. A large section of it is beginning to realize the community of its interests with those of the class which is capable of pointing the way out of the cul-de-sac.

Wells: You of all people know something about revolutions, Mr. Stalin, from the practical side. Do the masses ever rise? Is it not an established truth that all revolutions are made by a minority?

Stalin: To bring about a revolution a leading revolutionary minority is required; but the most talented, devoted and energetic minority would be helpless if it did not rely upon the at least passive support of millions.

Wells: At least passive? Perhaps sub-conscious?

Stalin: Partly also the semi-instinctive and semiconscious, but without the support of millions, the best minority is impotent.

Wells: I watch communist propaganda in the West and it seems to me that in modern conditions this propaganda sounds very oldfashioned, because it is insurrectionary propaganda. Propaganda in favor of the violent overthrow of the social system ,was all very well when it was directed against tyranny. But under modern conditions, when the system is collapsing anyhow, stress should be laid on efficiency, on competence, on productiveness, and not on insurrection. It seems to me that the insurrectionary note is obsolete. The communist propaganda in the West is a nuisance to constructive minded people.

Stalin: Of course the old system is breaking down, decaying. That is true. But it is also true that new efforts are being made by other methods, by every means, to protect, to save this dying system. You draw a wrong conclusion from a correct postulate. You rightly state that the old world is breaking down. But you are wrong in thinking that it is breaking down of its own accord No, the substitution of one social system for another is a complicated and long revolutionary process. It is not simply a spontaneous process, but a struggle, it is a process connected with the clash of classes. Capitalism is decaying, but it must not be compared simply with a tree which has decayed to such an extent that it must fall to the ground of its own accord. No, revolution, the substitution of one social system for another, has always been a struggle, a painful and a cruel struggle, a life and death struggle. And every time the people of the new world came into power, they had to defend themselves against the attempts of the old world to restore the old order by force; these people of the new world always had to be on the alert, always had to be ready to repel the attacks of the old world upon the new system.

Yes, you are right when you say that the old social system is breaking down; but it is not breaking down of its own accord. Take Fascism for example. Fascism is a reactionary force which is trying to preserve the old world by means of violence. What will you do with the fascists? Argue with them? Try to convince them? But this will have no effect upon them at all. Communists do not in the least idealize the methods of violence. But they, the Communists, do not want to be taken by surprise, they cannot count on the old world voluntarily departing from the stage, they see that the old system is violently defending itself, and that is why the Communists say to the working class: Answer violence with violence; do all you can to prevent the old dying order from crushing you, do ,not permit it to put manacles on your hands, on the hands with which you will overthrow the old system. As you see, the Communists regard the substitution of one social system for another, not simply as a spontaneous and peaceful process, but as a complicated, long and violent process. Communists cannot ignore facts.

Wells: But look at what is now going on in the capitalist world. The collapse is not a simple one: it is the outbreak of reactionary violence which is degenerating to gangsterism. And it seems to me that when it comes to a conflict with reactionary and unintelligent violence, socialists can appeal to the law, and instead of regarding the police as the enemy they should support them in the fight against the reactionaries. I think that it is useless operating with the methods of the old rigid insurrectionary socialism.

Stalin: The Communists base themselves on rich historical experience which teaches that obsolete classes do not voluntarily abandon the stage of history. Recall the history of England in the seventeenth century. Did not many say that the old social system had decayed? But did it not, nevertheless, require a Cromwell to crush it by force?

Wells: Cromwell operated on the basis of the constitution and in the name of constitutional order.

Stalin: In the name of the constitution he resorted to violence, beheaded the king, dispersed Parliament, arrested some and beheaded others! Or take an example from our history. Was it not clear for a long time that the tsarist system was decaying, was breaking down? But how much blood had to be shed in order to overthrow it? And what about the October Revolution? Were there not plenty of people who knew that we alone, the Bolsheviks, were indicating the only correct way out? Was it not clear that Russian capitalism had decayed? But you know how great was the resistance, how much blood had to be shed in order to defend the October Revolution from all its enemies, internal and external. Or take France at the end of the eighteenth century. Long before 1789 it was clear to many how rotten the royal power, the feudal system was. But a popular insurrection, a clash of classes was not, ,could not be avoided. Why? Because the classes which must abandon the stage of history are the last to become convinced that their role is ended. It is impossible to convince them of this. They think that the fissures in the decaying edifice of the old order can be mended, that the tottering edifice of the old order can be repaired and saved. That is why dying classes take to arms and resort to every means to save their existence as a ruling class.

Wells: But there were not a few lawyers at the head of the Great French Revolution.

Stalin: Do you deny the role of the intelligentsia in revolutionary movements? Was the Great French Revolution a lawyers' revolution and not a popular revolution, which achieved victory by rousing vast masses of the people against feudalism and championed the interests of the Third Estate? And did the lawyers among the leaders of the Great French Revolution act in accordance with the laws of the old order? Did they not introduce new, bourgeois-revolutionary laws? The rich experience of history teaches that up to now not a single class has voluntarily made way for another class. There is no such precedent in world history. The Communists have learned this lesson of history. Communists would welcome the voluntary departure of the bourgeoisie. But such a turn of affairs is improbable: that is what experience teaches. That is why the Communists want to be prepared for the worst and call upon the working class to be vigilant, to be prepared for battle. Who wants a captain who lulls the vigilance of his army, a captain who does not understand that the enemy will not surrender, that he must be crushed? To be such a captain means deceiving, betraying the working class. That is why I think that what seems to you to be old-fashioned is in fact a measure of revolutionary expediency for the working class.

Wells: I do not deny that force has to be used, but I think the forms of the struggle should fit as closely as possible to the opportunities presented by the existing laws, which must be defended against reactionary attacks. There is no need to disorganize the old system because it is' disorganizing itself enough as it is. That is why it seems to me insurrection against the old order, against the law, is<'obsolete, old-fashioned. Incidentally, I deliberately exaggerate in order to bring the truth out more clearly. I can formulate my point of view in the following way: first, I am for order; second, I attack the present system in so far as it cannot assure order: third, I think that class war propaganda may detach from socialism just those educated people whom socialism needs.

Stalin: In order to achieve a great object, an important social object, there must be a main force, a bulwark, a revolutionary class. Next it is necessary to organize the assistance of an auxiliary force for this main force: in this case this auxiliary force is the Party, to which the best forces of the intelligentsia belong. Just now you spoke about "educated people;" But what educated people did you have in mind? Were there not plenty of educated people on the side of the old order in England in the seventeenth century, in France at the end of the eighteenth century, and in Russia in the epoch of the October Revolution? The old order: had in its service many highly educated people who defended the old order, who opposed the new order. Education is a weapon the effect of which be struck down. Of course, the proletariat, socialism, needs is determined by the hands which wield it, by who is to highly educated people. Clearly, simpletons cannot help the proletariat to fight for socialism, to build a new society. I do not underestimate the role of the intelligentsia; on the contrary, emphasize it. The question is, however, which intelligentsia are we discussing? Because there are different kinds of intelligentsia.

Wells: There can be no revolution without a radical change in the educational system. It is sufficient to quote two examples: The example of the German Republic, which did not touch the old educational system, and therefore never became a republic: and the example of the British Labor Party, which lacks the determination to insist on a radical change in the educational system.

Stalin: That is a correct observation. Permit me now to reply to, your three points.

First, the main thing for the revolution is the existence of a social bulwark. This bulwark of the revolution is the working class.

Second, an auxiliary force is required, that which the Communists call a Party. To the Party belong the intelligent workers and those elements of the technical intelligentsia which are closely connected with the working class. The intelligentsia can be strong only if it combines with the working class. If it opposes the working class it becomes a cipher.

Third, political power is required as a lever for change. The new political power creates the new laws, the new order, which is revolutionary order.

I do not stand for any kind of order. I stand for order that corresponds to the interests of the working class. If however, any of the laws of the old order can be utilized in the interests of the struggle for the new order, the old laws should be utilized. I cannot object to your postulate that the present system should be attacked in so far as it does not insure the necessary order for the people.

And, finally, you are wrong if you think that the Communists are enamored with violence. They would be very pleased to drop violent methods if the ruling class agreed to give way to the working class. But the experience of history speaks against such an assumption.

Wells: There was a case in the history of England, however, of a class voluntarily handing over power to another class. In the period between 1830 and 1870, the aristocracy, whose influence was still very considerable at the end of the eighteenth century, voluntarily, without a severe struggle, surrendered power to the bourgeoisie, which serves as a sentimental support of the monarchy. Subsequently, this transference of power led to the establishment of the rule of the financial oligarchy.

Stalin: But you have imperceptibly passed from questions of revolution to questions of reform. This is not the same thing. Don't you think that the Chartist movement played a great role in the Reforms in England in the nineteenth century?

Wells: The Chartists did little and disappeared without leaving a trace.

Stalin: I do not agree with you. The Chartists, and the strike movement which they organized, played a great role; they compelled the ruling classes to make a number of concessions in regard to the franchise, in regard to abolishing the so-called "rotten boroughs," and in regard to some of the points of the "Charter." Chartism played a not unimportant historical role and compelled a section of the ruling classes to make certain concessions, reforms, in order to avert great shocks. Generally speaking, it must be said that of all the ruling classes, the ruling classes of England, both the aristocracy and the bourgeoisie, proved to be the cleverest, most flexible from the point of view of their class interests, from the point of view of maintaining their power. Take as an example, say, from modern history, the general strike in England in 1926. The first thing any other bourgeoisie would have done in the face. of such an event, when the General Council of Trade Unions called for a strike, would have been to arrest the trade union leaders. The British bourgeoisie did not do that, and it acted cleverly from the point of view of its own interests. I cannot conceive of such a flexible strategy being employed by the bourgeoisie in the United States, Germany or France. In order to maintain their rule, the ruling classes of Great Britain have never foresworn small concessions, reforms. But it would be a mistake to think that these reforms were revolutionary.

Wells: You have a higher opinion of the ruling classes of my country than I have. But is there a great difference between a small revolution and a great reform? Is not a reform a small revolution?

Stalin: Owing to pressure from below, the pressure of the masses, the bourgeoisie may sometimes concede certain partial reforms while remaining on the basis of the existing social-economic system. Acting in this way, it calculates that these concessions are necessary in order to preserve its class rule. This is the essence of reform. Revolution, however, means the transference of power from one class to another. That is why it is impossible to describe any reform as revolution. That is why we cannot count on the change of social systems taking place as an imperceptible transition from one system to another by means, of reforms, by the ruling class making concessions....

Wells: I am very grateful to you for this talk which has meant a great deal to me. In explaining things to me you probably called to mind how you had to explain the fundamentals of socialism in the illegal circles before the revolution. At the present time there are in the world only two persons to whose opinion, to whose every word, millions are listening: you and Roosevelt. Others may preach as much as they like; what they say will never be printed or heeded. I cannot yet appreciate what has been done in your country; I only arrived yesterday. But I have already seen the happy faces of healthy men and women and I know that something very considerable is being done here. The contrast with 1920 is astounding.

Stalin: Much more could have been done had we Bolsheviks been cleverer.

Wells: No, if human beings were cleverer it would be a good thing to invent a five-year plan for the reconstruction of the human brain which obviously lacks many things needed for a perfect social order. (Laughter).

Stalin: Don't you intend to stay for the Congress of the Soviet Writers Union?

Wells: Unfortunately, I have various engagements to fulfill and can stay in the U.S.S.R. only for a week. I came to see you and I am very satisfied by our talk. But I intend to discuss with such Soviet writers as I can meet the possibility of their affiliating to the P.E.N. club. This is an international organization of writers founded by Galsworthy; after his death I became president. The organization is still weak, but it has branches in many countries, and what is more important, the speeches of its members, are widely reported in the press. It insists upon this free expression of opinion, even of opposition opinion. I hope to discuss this point with Gorky. I do not know if you are prepared yet for that much freedom here.

Stalin: We Bolsheviks call it "self-criticism." It is widely used in the U.S.S.R. If there is anything I can do to help you I shall be glad to do so.

Wells: (Expresses thanks.)

Stalin: (Expresses thanks for the visit.)

A List of H. G Wells Books in this Series

FICTION

A Modern Utopia

Babes in the Darkling Wood - A Novel of Ideas

Boon, The Mind of the Race, The Wild Asses of the Devil, and The Last Trump

In the Days of the Comet

Kipps: The Story of a Simple Soul

Men Like Gods

Star-Begotten - A Biological Fantasia

The Autocracy of Mr. Parham - His Remarkable Adventures in This Changing World

The BrothersThe Camford Visitation

The Croquet Player

The Dream

The Fight in the Lion's Thicket

The First Horseman

The First Men in the Moon

The Grisly Folk

The Holy Terror

The Invisible Man

The King Who Was a King - The Book of a Film

The Land Ironclads

The New Machiavelli

The Passionate Friends

The Pearl of Love

The Queer Story of Brownlow's Newspaper

The Red Room

The Reign of Uya the Lion

The Research Magnificent

The Sea Lady

The Secret Places of the Heart

The Shape of Things to Come

The Sleeper Awakes - A Revised Edition of When the Sleeper Wakes

The Soul of a Bishop

The Time Machine

The Undying Fire

The War in the Air

The War of the Worlds

The Wife of Sir Isaac Harman

The Wild Asses of the Devil

The Wonderful Visit

The World Set Free

Ugh-Lomi and the Cave Bear

Ugh-Lomi and Uya

When the Sleeper Wakes

You Can't Be Too Careful

A List of H. G Wells Books in this Series

FICTION COLLECTIONS

The Short Stories of H. G. Wells

Tales of Space and Time

The Country of the Blind, and Others

The Door in the Wall, and Others

The Plattner Story and Others

The Stolen Bacillus and Others

The Time Machine and Others

Twelve Stories and a Dream

NON-FICTION

A Year of Prophesying

Anticipations

Certain Personal Matters

Crux Ansata

Experiment in Autobiography

First and Last Things: A Confession of Faith and Rule of Life

God, the Invisible King

Mankind in the Making

Marxism vs. Liberalism - An Interview

Mr. Belloc Objects to "The Outline of History"

New Worlds For Old: A Plain Account of Modern Socialism

Scientific War

Select Conversations with an Uncle (Now Extinct) and Two Other Reminiscences

Socialism and the Family

Text Book of Biology, Part 1: Vertebrata

The Anatomy of Frustration

The Common Sense of War and Peace

The Discovery of the Future

The Elements of Reconstruction

The Future in America

The Idea of a League of Nations

The Salvaging of Civilization

The Story of a Great Schoolmaster

The War That Will End War

This Misery of Boots (1907)

War and the Future:

What is Coming? A Forecast of Things after the War

World Brain

Printed in Great Britain
by Amazon